To find out more about the Universal Design Method and how you can incorporate it in your life, please visit my website:

LauraMineff.com

A ROUND PEG IN A SQUARE WORLD

Designing New Opportunities in a World of Infinite Possibilities

Laura Mineff

THiNK*aha*®

An Actionable Success Journal

E-mail: info@thinkaha.com
20660 Stevens Creek Blvd., Suite 210
Cupertino, CA 95014

Please go to
https://aha.pub/BeARoundPeg
to read this AHAbook and to share the
individual AHAmessages that resonate with you.

Published by THiNKaha®
20660 Stevens Creek Blvd., Suite 210,
Cupertino, CA 95014
https://thinkaha.com
E-mail: info@thinkaha.com

First Printing: March 2021
Hardcover ISBN: 978-1-61699-375-7   1-61699-375-8
Paperback ISBN: 978-1-61699-374-0   1-61699-374-X
eBook ISBN: 978-1-61699-375-7   1-61699-375-8
Place of Publication: Silicon Valley, California, USA
Paperback Library of Congress Number: 2020922707

Trademarks

Warning and Disclaimer

DEDICATION

My mom has been my greatest friend and teacher over the last fifty years. She has truly allowed me to experiment with life in an unconditional atmosphere. This has been invaluable to finding and enjoying my true self. I know that we have both embraced this beautiful gift of unconditional love and acceptance, followed by great appreciation for each other.

> *Mom, your words and actions have been an inspiration and beautiful guidance in my life. I couldn't have had the adventure of finding my joyful bliss without our relationship.*

I am so appreciative of the beautiful, creative insight of my daughter Lindsey. She truly brought these pages to life and was a continuous inspiration for me to keep moving.

> *My great love to both of you. Thank you.*

ACKNOWLEDGEMENTS

Thank you to the beautiful life guides throughout my journey for allowing me to openly share the magic and the flow of joy in this loving, human life experience. You have shown me the true secret of creating my own life adventures. We are meant to create our own reality, and the voices in our heads attract us to our life focuses, fears, and thoughts.

Chicke Fitzgerald, without your guidance, I could not have gotten my messages, my thoughts, and my heart into this manuscript.

The rest of you, you know who you are.

Thank you. You know how much you mean to me.

How to Read a THiNKaha® Book

A Note from the Publisher

The AHAthat/THiNKaha series was crafted to deliver content the way humans process information in today's world. Short, sweet, and to the point while delivering powerful, lasting impact.

The content is designed and presented in ways to appeal to visual, auditory, and kinesthetic personality types. Each section contains AHAmessages, lines for notes, and a meme that summarizes that section. You should also scan the QR code, or click on the link, to watch a video of Laura talking about that section.

This book is contextual in nature. Although the words won't change, their meaning will every time you read it as your context will. Be ready, you will experience your own AHA moments as you read. The AHA messages are designed to be stand-alone actionable messages that will help you think differently. Items to consider as you're reading include:

1. It should only take less than two hours to read the first time. When you're reading, write one to three action items that resonate with you in the underlined areas.

2. Mark your calendar to re-read it again.

3. Repeat step #1 and mark one to three additional AHA messages that resonate. As they will most likely be different, this is a great time to reflect on the messages that resonated with you during your last reading.

4. Sprinkle credust on the author and yourself by sharing the AHA messages from this book socially from the AHAthat platform https://aha.pub/BeARoundPeg.

After reading this THiNKaha book, marking your AHA messages, re-reading it, and marking more AHA messages, you'll begin to see how this book contextually applies to you. We advocate for continuous, lifelong learning and this book will help you transform your AHAs into action items with tangible results.

Mitchell Levy, Global Credibility Expert
publisher@thinkaha.com

THiNKaha®

A THiNKaha book is not your typical book. It's a whole lot more, while being a whole lot less. Scan the QR code or use this link to watch me talk about this new evolutionary style of book: https://aha.pub/THiNKahaSeries.

CONTENTS

PROLOGUE

Throughout my life, there were several moments that guided me to change how I approach living. My ex-husband, George, was a main catalyst that inspired a huge change in my life.

He and I met when he was still in law school. He graduated and started his own practice, and we raised four beautiful children together for sixteen years before we divorced.

My ex-husband was an attorney with his own practice. He would get up and go to work at 7 am every day and would often work late into the night and on weekends. As with many living this routine, he thought his demanding and high-paying job made him successful. He, like so many others, thought that money would buy him happiness and love. This was an idea passed on from father to son through many generations—that is, until my son came along.

My ex took care of the kids the only way he knew how. He paid for anything that would set them up for success in society by his definition. He paid their full college tuition, graduate school, a reliable vehicle, etc. He considered this a success and sent them off on their own, and that was it.

After the divorce, my second oldest son, Nicholas, took on the "man role" of the family. Nicholas made sure that all the other children were happy and kept the peace. He went on to law school and landed himself a job with his "successful" father.

George started Nicholas off on a very modest salary, but Nicholas made the most of it and got himself a roommate and made other budget adjustments to make the low salary work.

For over twenty years, Nicholas had watched his dad miss major family functions and work himself into major health issues. He watched as his dad worked endless hours so we could have a nice house, health insurance, and other provisions. His dad never dropped that ball of responsibility, but he had high expectations for Nicholas to do the same.

After working with his dad for a year, Nicholas came to the conclusion that he could not work to live. He didn't want to work late into the evenings and on weekends. He found the value in enjoying life's experiences and wanted to seize that opportunity.

He approached his dad and said, *"Dad, I love you and I appreciate the opportunities that you've given me. I'm appreciative of this job that I'm doing today, but I am not going to be like you. I cannot work to live. I want work to provide myself with the income to enjoy life. I will not be working on Saturdays and Sundays. I'll come in at 8 but at 5:30, I'm going to go home."*

His dad was rattled. Although that was seven years ago, to this day, they still disagree on this topic. He couldn't relate to Nicholas' need to live his life a different way and just thought that Nicholas was lazy and didn't care.

- People seem to be **#conditioned** to think that their way is the best way and that everyone should see their way of doing things. This conditioning can hinder them from achieving a happier and healthier life.

Nicholas was brave to live his truth and break away from his father's shadow. I truly believe this statement.

- With the simplest of adjustments, you can create a new path and journey for yourself. Life is all about the journey and having the **#courage** to take it.

We find ourselves at different stages throughout our life journey. Regardless of the era when we were born, all of us are given the freedom to choose the path that we desire.

- Beautiful **#opportunities** come to people all the time! You just need to crack open the door of your mind to be awakened to these opportunities.

This learning was the catalyst for the creation of the Universal Design Method that you will read about in this book. It is a mixture of changing your physical environment and your mindset and guiding you toward the joy of life.

INTRODUCTION

When I met Laura Mineff, what struck me immediately was her countenance. I realize that isn't a word that is frequently used in the English language, but it is by far the best word to describe my first encounter with her.

Laura seems to actually "transmit" joy—it is in her eyes, her words, and definitely in her laugh and her ever-present smile. I felt welcomed into her world, and even though we hadn't known each other long, I felt like I could trust her and that I could tell her literally anything and that she would understand.

This is a book that is written for those who want to live in a place where they can find solace and serenity. And quite frankly, it is for those who would like to be described the way I just described Laura.

It is likely that you are facing change in your life. You could be nearing retirement, perhaps you were a part of a downsizing in your company, you may have parents who may need more care in the coming years, or you are facing a breakup, becoming an empty nester, or dealing with the loss of a spouse.

So many struggle to find joy, especially in these turbulent times. They need to find courage and learn to communicate more freely, more honestly and more openly.

If only you could change the atmosphere around you, find peace in the midst of chaos, and have clarity about the direction that you should take!

You can! It is attainable. Through this book, Laura will walk you through a practical methodology to break down restraining barriers, seen and unseen, so you can see the opportunities and options and positively move on to the next chapter in your life.

She will teach you how to design your life and your environment. She will show you how tell your story and demonstrate ways to add value to others' lives.

Artist Mary Engelbreit said, *"If you don't like something, change it; if you can't change it, change the way you think about it."* That is Laura's Universal Design Method in a nutshell.

Embrace it. Live it. Release fear. Radiate joy.

Be willing to be a round peg in a square world.

CHICKE FITZGERALD
CEO & Founder
Solutionz Innovations and the Game Changer Network

People are #conditioned to think that they are better & smarter than others and even entitled. This conditioning can hinder them from achieving a happier & healthier life.

LAURA MINEFF
https://Aha.pub/BeARoundPeg

Share the AHA messages from this book socially by going to
https://aha.pub/BeARoundPeg.

Scan the QR code or use this link to watch the section videos and more on this section topic:
https://aha.pub/BeARoundPegSVs

SECTION I

Appreciating the vortex.

Have you ever asked yourself how we have been conditioned to act the way we do?

When we enter this human experience, beginning with our first breath, we emerge from a perfect, beautiful, safe space, bathed in pure love and pure joy, ready for adventure. That love and joy form a metaphorical cocoon, where we reside until we can emerge on our own, strong and ready to fly.

At that moment, our path lies before us, full of curves, twists and turns, and infinite possibilities. We are born with everything that we need for the journey that we call life.

Then, without warning, the conditioning begins. Those who surround us inflict their conditional thought processes and their ways on us. Throughout our lives, it is these external influences that actually help us sort through things to find our own identity and establish our own mindset.

In those early days, we are surrounded by those charged with raising us. This is normally your parents. But it may be those who actually volunteered for that role— siblings, other family members and care givers, teachers, and mentors. They influence our lives, and we are shaped by the choices they make, including their reactions to adversity and even to the good things in life.

Are you one of the fortunate ones who were surrounded with one or more people caring for and nurturing you in your early years? If so, you will know those individuals breathed life into you through their model of unconditional love. If not, don't lose heart. It doesn't have to define your story.

Even if the intentions of your caregivers were good, their guidance is fueled by their own individual life challenges and experiences. They project their thoughts, including their fears, a sense of lack, and their insecurities.

Clearly, some of that influence can also be positive, but most often, that conditioning causes us to put up barriers and walls that unwittingly can make our world square, boxed in, and more difficult to navigate. Fortunately, these lessons can also be our greatest teacher if we can recognize the habits and our environment for what they are and see how they impact our lives.

As we grow up, our world is continually shaped by our physical environment and surroundings and what we draw to ourselves, reflecting how we are treated and nurtured emotionally (. . . or not).

During adolescence, a child formulates their view of themselves from this conditioning. Figuratively, they begin to find their wings and push against the protective cocoon. This is often seen as their first act of rebellion. But no one can open the cocoon on our behalf. There are just some things that have to happen from the inside out at their appointed time and this is one of them.

Like a scratch on an old vinyl record, the thoughts and actions of those around us can create grooves and scratches in our perfectly round world, almost immediately impacting our physical life experience. We need to recognize that these habitual thought processes can suck the life from us and cause us to erect walls of restriction.

Once we realize what is happening, it can become a circular, swirling vortex of unlimited resources. The realizations that emanate from that energy are what equip us to break free from the constraints of our physical reality, just like a rocket breaking free from orbit.

The influences in our life clarify what we do and do not want to bring into our life experience. After we learn the lesson, we must shed those influences and move forward. Then, we are free to achieve breakthrough and discover our true selves.

Once again, we become that innocent, beautiful butterfly, full of love and joy and childlike wonder, where anything is possible.

Enter stage left, the ego.

It is not unusual at this point to believe that you are better and smarter than others and even that you are entitled. There are many manifestations of this entitlement. The ego imposes itself on our behavior and influences and manipulates our responses. It also influences how we communicate and receive information.

The ego can easily be seen as the monster in the story—the devil sitting on our shoulder. His job is pointing out the things that we can't do and all of the things we aren't (smart enough, thin enough, rich enough), and his goal is making everything all about us. This robs us of the joy that was God's intended plan for our life.

It is normal to want to be the beautiful butterfly, and loving. We can't respect one another if we don't love and respect ourselves. This comes out of operating in the fear of not being worthy, accepted, or loved. Instead of breaking out of the cocoon and stepping into what we were created to be, we remain imprisoned, as if in a cage.

We desire to be acknowledged and appreciated. To do that, we need to learn how to move aside our fears, to find the way to unveil our pure motives and embrace our potential. Through our own appreciation of ourselves and in freely loving ourselves, we can come to show pure love to others.

Only when we have an appreciation of what the ego points out to us can we make peace with it and have an appreciation for that early conditioning and even for the swirling vortex. We are then equipped to remove the resistance and see the opportunities to choose from, directing our own path.

Only at that point can we hear the "voice" of and operate in pure love. That voice tells us that we matter, that we are indeed worthy, and that we can do and be anything. By receiving and being empowered with that knowledge as we venture out and listen to others and appreciate their stories, we can then understand, interact, and truly care.

When we discover the courage and bravery within, we can see the accusing character on our shoulder as the clarifier, the one who keeps us on our toes and helps us to reflect our true nature in the choices we make.

When we alleviate our fears and tune our ego, we open up to others and to the world, and we begin to soften our edges. We also find a new joy in participating in life and can accept that we are the creators of our own reality. We have options and there are infinite possibilities.

I created the Universal Design Method to address the challenge created by this conditioning. It is designed to create a space where you feel empowered. In some cases, it literally lights your path. It is geared to enable you to live a happier and healthier life.

Reconditioning your mindset and shifting your environment can enable you to find the happiness and embrace the manifestation of your true nature and have a joyful life.

By reading this book and discovering your own AHA! moments, together, we are designing new opportunities in a world of infinite possibilities and helping you enjoy being a round peg in that square world.

1

People are #conditioned to think that they are better and smarter than others and even entitled. This conditioning can hinder them from achieving a happier and healthier life.

_____

_____

_____

2

What's blocking a person's #conditioning? Think about it. Does it reflect one's true nature as a loving and caring human being?

_____

_____

_____

3

People want to be loved, accepted, appreciated, and acknowledged. They try to seek this out in others instead of looking into themselves and their #surroundings. #conditioning

_____

_____

_____

4

Do people sincerely care? Yes, they do. It is just a matter of opening their hearts and minds to others. The #UniversalDesignMethod is designed to open spaces that help open one's mind by #releasing the #joy of #life. #conditioning

_____

_____

_____

5

A person's true nature is to be caring, loving, and playful. The #UniversalDesignMethod releases the energy to reflect this through the #ease and flow of incorporating curved design. #conditioning

_____

_____

_____

6

When people set their egos aside, their true human nature emerges. Through the #UniversalDesignMethod, people can start discovering their true nature of being open to others by just letting go. #conditioning

_____

_____

_____

7

The #UniversalDesignMethod can create a path that allows people to be self-reflective on their successes so they can share the newfound sense of self-worthiness with society. #conditioning

---

8

The #UniversalDesignMethod is a methodology that can enable a person to live a more #loving and #joyful and #healthier life. It allows them to move aside fear and have the #courage to see things differently. #UDM

9

The path to true happiness is always through a loving
heart. #conditioning #unconditionallove

_____

_____

_____

10

The most important person to love is one's self. People
can only give what they have. To love another, one must
first love one's self. To appreciate another, one must first
appreciate one's self. #conditioning

_____

_____

_____

11

When people release their fears, the walls go down and they become open and appreciative of others. The #UniversalDesignMethod releases one's inner restrictions by moving the #energy, softening the edges, in order to enjoy who one's self is. #conditioning

_____

_____

_____

12

Do you know the biggest fear that people have is feeling that they are not worthy anymore? This can be addressed by a change of #mindset, which is vital for people to find the joy in their self-worth.

_____

_____

_____

13

Do you know that the #UniversalDesignMethod can provide the support that you need when you experience a #change in your life? It acts by altering one's atmosphere to reflect and encourage the change.

_____

_____

_____

14

Living in the moment is a mindset where people appreciate the place they are in right now. How can you best appreciate the place you are currently in? #livinginthemoment

_____

_____

_____

15

The #UniversalDesignMethod can influence emotions because it alters the atmosphere and touches one's spirit. #change

_____

_____

_____

16

People need to recall what brought them #joy and only then can they #freely share this joy with others, letting it resonate in their very being. This is the fun part of the journey!

_____

_____

_____

17

The #UniversalDesignMethod creates that mindset of openness and giving back to society. What have you given back to others? #journey

_____

_____

_____

18

#Joy flows when people connect to God as their energy source and the source of provision. The #UniversalDesignMethod allows one to feel connected to that free-flowing, unconditional love.

_____

_____

_____

19

When people discover themselves through the help of the #UniversalDesignMethod, they are able to move forward and positively influence their life and the lives of others. #conditioning

_____

_____

_____

20

Practitioners of the #UniversalDesignMethod have a desire to add value to society. They have an appreciation for where they have come from and where they are today. #journey

_____

_____

_____

People inherently know when it is
time to make a #change.
All they need is a nudge. Sometimes,
they also have to give #permission to
take that next step to a loving & happy life.

LAURA MINEFF
https://Aha.pub/BeARoundPeg

Share the AHA messages from this book socially by going to
https://aha.pub/BeARoundPeg.

*Scan the QR code or use this link to watch the
section videos and more on this section topic:*
https://aha.pub/BeARoundPegSVs

SECTION II

Are your "spidey senses" signaling it is time for a change?

There are many times in your life when you need to make changes – opening up or just creating the crack of insight to see your way through life's challenges, embracing the lessons along the way.

I know from experience that God never gives you more than you can handle. He will always provide a way out so you can endure it, because that is His nature, which never changes.

The catalysts for change come in many forms, and there are generally clear signs. Sometimes it is just a tap on the shoulder, and sometimes it is a wrecking ball.

If you can't look in the mirror and appreciate your value, that's a telltale sign. If you are sad, or you're angry and defensive; if you feel confused by what to do next; if you are depressed or facing a huge change, these too are signals. If you feel isolated, lonely, and alienated, you are ready for a shift in thought patterns, allowing you to see and appreciate your own value and find your warrior shield to connect to the power of love and joy.

It is not just the negative emotions and actions that call for change. When you have a new love in your life, when you have a child, or when you are excited about a new opportunity or move to a new home or office, in order to tune in and tap into those good feelings, you must change your sensory environment or initiate changes in your responses to your situation. If you don't, you will hold back the positive impact of the new situation and miss out on experiencing the joy of the journey.

Appreciation for yourself and your new situation is the key to finding the joy in living. When you make that discovery, you inspire others, and your newfound enthusiasm can spill over to them.

It is important to recognize that there are generational differences, both in openness and in embracing a shift in your physical environment and changing the way you react. The younger generation has access to information available at their fingertips, yet they lack the life experience to apply that knowledge. Technology and the speed of communication is a big shift for the older generation. This creates the fear of being left behind and can impact their adoption of new things and ideas.

No matter what your age, there will always be more information flowing than you can possibly absorb. Let go of the extra minutia. It just gets in the way and throws us off our true path.

So, is it time for a change?

Trust yourself. Allow the answer to be "yes," and embrace the change. It is time to get started on making and embracing a joyful, fun, and adventurous life. It is time to tune in and tap into the possibilities.

Embracing the Universal Design Method helps move you through that process of change in your life—teaching you how to relax and not take everything personally, knowing that each day is a new set of opportunities.

It helps you learn to have that love for yourself to move forward. It teaches you how to enhance the lives of others along your journey, participating in the well-being of our community and our world and even our universe.

The methodology that I share with you in this book addresses the needs and preferences of any age group, and as a result, it can be a bridge between generations, as it naturally draws like-minded individuals together. And together, we are creating the next amazing chapter in our history.

21

People inherently know when it is time to make a #change. All they need is a nudge. Sometimes, they also have to give themselves #permission to take that next step to a loving and happier life.

_____

_____

_____

22

When it's time for a #change, people feel an unrelenting desire to have something different in their lives.

_____

_____

_____

23

People know it is time for a #change when something in their world doesn't fit anymore. When they recognize that their circumstances have changed, it is time to trust themselves by finding the courage to embrace change.

_____

_____

_____

24

Addressing one's fear can be motivated by a catalyst. Catalysts act like triggers to start a #newmindset.

_____

_____

_____

25

When a catalyst happens, people are compelled to
change because they now have a completely different
outlook. #newmindset

_____

_____

_____

26

New responsibilities can be catalysts for people to
change their #mindsets without even being aware of it.
What new responsibilities do you face?

_____

_____

_____

27

Technology and the speed of communication is a big shift for the older generation. This creates the fear of being left behind. People have a choice to #change and adjust to letting go of old ways or continue to live in fear!

28

The younger generation has access to info available at their fingertips. Through technology, they know more innately than any other generation, but they do not know how to apply their skilled knowing into practical experience. #Change

29

The pace of information exchange is ever increasing. If people try to learn everything at once, they will never catch up. Let go of the extra minutia. It just gets in the way and throws us off our true path.

30

When people don't recognize that it's time to make a #change, they can start to feel stuck, trapped, wronged, insignificant, and hopeless. The only way to shift this #paradigm is to redirect their focus.

31

When people can look in the mirror and love and appreciate themselves, they open up to #change and find #pure joy. It's time to find a good #mantra—one for the beginning of the day and for the end of the day.

_____

_____

_____

32

People cannot give what they don't have. They must first have #respect, #love, #worthiness, #appreciation, and #honor within themselves before they can share them with others.

_____

_____

_____

33

The #UniversalDesignMethod creates a synergy that connects everything and in turn, connects everyone. And it draws like-minded people to each other. #change

_____

_____

_____

34

The #UniversalDesignMethod curves out the energy, creating a flow for people to dwell in and find a new perspective of how to live. It creates the ability to open up to the options for change and pick a new life experience.

_____

_____

_____

35

The younger generation is focused on the actual journey and adventure. The older generation is focused on the end result. There is a benefit in appreciating both #mindsets.

_____

_____

_____

36

As you get older, you fear being left behind and not being worthy. The #UniversalDesignMethod allows people to apply their modern outlook in life to enhance the lives of others. If you're breathing, you're not done yet! #change

_____

_____

_____

37

People tend to stick to what they know. They may not be motivated to recognize their need to #change. The #UniversalDesignMethod gives a new perspective to get people unstuck. Let go of boring old #habits and grasp onto new exciting ones.

_____

_____

_____

38

Why do people feel stuck? It's because they tend to repeat their habitual routine out of fear of the unknown. The #UniversalDesignMethod can help people get unstuck by creating new excitement in their thinking and environment. #change

_____

_____

_____

39

When people have habits that no longer benefit them, it is time for a #change. The #UniversalDesignMethod breaks those habits through disrupting current patterns in your environment.

_____

_____

_____

40

People often don't know how to take that next step in their lives because they can't see what it is. They need to unleash their resistance to the unknown in order to figure out how to move forward. #change

_____

_____

_____

41

Why is it difficult for people to move forward? This is because their environment remains the same. With the #UniversalDesignMethod, even small additions and/or alterations can open people up to #change.

_____

_____

_____

42

It does not take a major #change in one's home or workplace to make them feel good about the changes in life. Even little adjustments can make a huge impact!

_____

_____

_____

43

People can be too focused on the future. They need to discover the joy of #livinginthemoment.

_____

_____

_____

44

When people are open to others, they are reminded that everyone is connected. No one #journeys alone.

_____

_____

_____

45

The universe responds to what one focuses on. You can focus on the positive—#changing your focus can help you live happier and healthier. With #thelawofattraction, what we focus on is what we draw to ourselves.

_____

_____

_____

At any given moment, people can create a
new path & journey for themselves,
Life is all about the joy of the journey
& having the #courage to take it.

LAURA MINEFF
https://Aha.pub/BeARoundPeg

Share the AHA messages from this book socially by going to
https://aha.pub/BeARoundPeg.

*Scan the QR code or use this link to watch the
section videos and more on this section topic:*
https://aha.pub/BeARoundPegSVs

SECTION III

Where do you find the courage to take the next step?

Change happens when you develop a heightened awareness of what is going on around you. You are then wide open to recognizing the catalysts and triggers that reveal themselves. This compels you to take the next step in designing your life.

Let's look at a physical design example.

Imagine you are entering a new home. In the foyer, the flooring has been installed diagonally. You pause and then realize that you expected the floorboards to run vertically, leading visually to the back of the house, because that is what you are used to. But as you take it all in, you realize that the new layout makes you feel good, and the diagonal perspective actually leads your eyes in new directions that you may have previously missed with the old pattern.

Your feelings and responses are your guide, and they provide the courage to change. Trust those instincts. They have been there from the beginning. They are your emotional tuning fork. Use them to tune in and tap into the trust. Use your senses to initiate breakthrough – removing resistance. Like the new layout of the flooring, your life path is yours to organize and as a result, create new experiences.

Physically, when laying a floor, you can experiment. If the diagonal points to a wall, it is obvious even to the non-design professional that it would stifle creativity and the flow of energy around you. Turn them the other direction, and you will feel the release of what was inhibiting you. The new way just "feels right."

Similarly, from an emotional perspective, as you find the courage to experiment, you will see opportunities materialize right in front of you. If you can let go of the past, the walls will gradually come down, and your path will become clear. You will then see the infinite options.

You can then be confident in your decision and stick to it — seeing it through to the desired end result.

There are no wrongs, just definitions of what you enjoy and what you do not want in your life experience. Letting go and believing is the answer. You don't need any more strength than that.

You've got this!

When you begin to experiment and envision a new direction for your life, you need to support it by altering your surroundings, thought processes, personal habits, and responses.

Deploying the Universal Design Method reframes your outlook by giving you a different perspective. The key is in moving the energy, keeping life interesting and engaging, which results in pure joy.

As you adopt this method, it alters your environment to help you release your inhibitions and fears.

Explore. Find your own story. This will lead you to find the courage to take the next step toward a happier and healthier life.

A life of great joy.

46

At any given moment, people can create a new path and journey for themselves. Life is all about the joy of the journey and having the #courage to take it.

_____

_____

_____

47

Everybody receives a little message that it is time for a change. The #catalyst is different for everyone. But until people get it, it will enter into their lives over and over again, until it gets their attention and gets you to let go.

_____

_____

_____

48

When something challenging or catastophic happens in people's lives, it becomes no longer a choice but a requirement to recognize and make a #change.

_____

_____

_____

49

When people recognize catalysts or triggers, they find the #courage to embrace the change. What are the catalysts in your life?

_____

_____

_____

50

When people are up against a wall and feel like they don't have any choice but to make a change, they can then find the #courage to face it.

_____

_____

_____

51

People are programmed that there is a right way and a wrong way to do life. There are no wrongs in life, only consequences to the choices made. These choices are lessons that can #change people's mindsets and open them up to a new path.

_____

_____

_____

52

People's #courage surfaces when they are able to let go of what inhibits them from seeing the opportunities right in front of them.

_____

_____

_____

53

Finding the #courage to change comes with heightened awareness of one's surroundings. The #UniversalDesignMethod heightens awareness by drawing one's attention to the beauty and energy in their surroundings, tapping into one's #seritonin.

_____

_____

_____

54

People must be open to something new, subsiding the fear, in order to find the #courage to connect with people who offer opportunities for change.

_____

_____

_____

55

Pay attention to others who are in the exact same situation but are taking a different direction. The oneness and connecting can stimulate you to find the desired #courage to change.

_____

_____

_____

56

When people are open and ready for change and the catalyst comes, they will easily find the #courage to change.

_____

_____

_____

57

Have you heard of being in the right place at the right time? This is not coincidence. This happens when your doors are open. The #UniversalDesignMethod helps open the doors of the mind to see opportunities. #courage

_____

_____

_____

58

Being a round peg in a square world is #empowering.
Step out and be emboldened by your new perspective.

_____

_____

_____

59

Do you have the #courage to be with a new person or have a new lifestyle? Finding the courage requires not focusing on the past, but letting it go.

_____

_____

_____

60

Practitioners of the #UniversalDesignMethod follow a methodology that allows them to generate the #courage they need to embrace the next step.

_____

_____

_____

61

When people feel connected to the flow of energy, they can trust themselves to find the #courage to take the next step in life. The #UniversalDesignMethod promotes that energy flow in its designs.

_____

_____

_____

62

People can only #change their own selves. They shouldn't blame others for how they feel about their words and actions. It's more than forgiveness, it's the ability to not take anything personally.

_____

_____

_____

63

When people are motivated or stimulated, that's when #courage arises for them to take the next step in life. The #UniversalDesignMethod stimulates people's minds and motivates them in the direction to make a change.

_____

_____

_____

64

Let go of the ideas of yesterday. Doing so creates happiness and joy and sets you up for future success. Have the #courage to let go!

_____

_____

_____

When people give thought to a new way of
functioning within their lives,
a breakthrough happens.
This is an exciting discovery for your journey!
#newmindset

LAURA MINEFF
https://Aha.pub/BeARoundPeg

Share the AHA messages from this book socially by going to
https://aha.pub/BeARoundPeg.

Scan the QR code or use this link to watch the
section videos and more on this section topic:
https://aha.pub/BeARoundPegSVs

SECTION IV

Creating a new mindset and releasing the fear.

Your mindset today is the result of the habitual grooves from the thought processes developed through your early conditioning. They are further carved through a wide variety of life experiences, including the repetitive and conditional reactions to events in your life.

There are no right or wrong reactions, but there are consequences to every choice we make.

How you receive information and respond to others contributes to your paradigm and can instill fear or release it. When you move aside the fear, it sets the tone for a new thought process. Releasing fear is only possible when you change your mindset.

In order for you to actively design a different life experience, you need to start with a reset of your thought processes. Eventually, this creates new habits.

The journey of changing your mindset begins with finding the courage to see things differently and make different decisions. This is an essential step to take in order to achieve an exciting, joyful, playful, and loving life.

Throughout the process, you must pay attention to all your senses. As you shift into a new pattern, your senses will follow and create a new direction.

The good news is that you can begin again at any moment. Every morning is new and that in itself is liberating.

Once you create a new mindset, you can begin inspiring others and continuing your own self expansion—pouring out more and more love and joy.

My cup runneth over . . .

In doing that, you are actively participating in and contributing to the wellbeing of mankind.

It begins with you.

The Universal Design Method was crafted to help you release your compartmentalized fear and find courage to modify your environment, seeing and opening up the possibilities. I want to encourage you to just do it. Embrace it!

Everyone feels at some point that they have a contribution to make. The methodology helps you to follow your heart. This gives you the courage to step out and onto your desired path, embrace your gifts, and experience the joy of sharing them with others.

65

The journey of changing one's #mindset begins with finding the courage to see things differently and make different decisions.

_____

_____

_____

66

The most beautiful thing that people can offer is to love unconditionally and to be nonjudgmental toward others. #joy

_____

_____

_____

67

The unknown can create fear. This should not stop people from embarking on this journey. Subsiding the fear opens one up to the whole world! #newmindset

_____

_____

_____

68

A #newmindset can be stimulated by fear, but did you know that this allows people to see things in a new light? Fear needs to be addressed in order to experience a beneficial turning point in your life.

_____

_____

_____

69

Everyone feels at some point that they have a contribution to make. The #UniversalDesignMethod helps people figure out what their talents are. This gives them the courage to step out and create their heart's desire. #newmindset.

70

When people open up to one another, they can find the courage to alter their future. Whom can you collaborate with to change the future? #newmindset

_____

_____

_____

71

The #UniversalDesignMethod helps people find #joy by addressing their fears. One's environment can be modified to take the fear away.

_____

_____

_____

72

People may need to shift their #paradigm so they appreciate the value in others. What is your current paradigm? #change

_____

_____

_____

73

Some people choose to live in fear because it is their habit of thought. The #UniversalDesignMethod helps people let go of their fears. It sets them on the path to finding their freedom to appreciate life. #newmindset

_____

_____

_____

74

When people move their fears aside, it sets the tone for a new thought process. The new thought process becomes like a rolling snowball in new snow. #newmindset

_____

_____

_____

75

When people release their fears, they will have the ability to expand mentally, physically, psychologically, lovingly, and universally. #newmindset

_____

_____

_____

76

People's #mindsets are created by the grooves carved on their thought processes. The grooves are formed by the experiences and the habits they have accumulated

_____

_____

_____

77

Many minor catalysts exist, but they don't change the grooves on one's thought process. An extension is simply added to that groove every time a minor catalyst is encountered. #newmindset

---

78

Do you know that when a new groove is carved into your mind, a new habit is formed? What new habits have you developed lately? #newmindset

_____

_____

_____

79

People are creatures of habit. Every morning, they get up and there is a routine that they follow. The grooves in their thought processes determine what they do every day . . . until they get #bored. #newmindset

_____

_____

_____

80

A person's routine can run for many years. They do not have to consciously think about it because it happens automatically. A change in that routine creates a new #mindset.

_____

_____

_____

81

With a #newmindset, people tend to start altering their approach to life in little ways. The #UniversalDesignMethod provides an outlet for people to alter their immediate surroundings, stimulating a new desire, a new thought pattern.

_____

_____

_____

82

In order for people to have a different life experience, they should find a way to reset their #mindsets. The #UniversalDesignMethod can help people create new grooves to reset their thinking.

_____

_____

_____

83

People can become so habitual about their life that when their atmosphere is rearranged through the #UniversalDesignMethod, it creates a whole different path in their minds to connect to their #joy.

_____

_____

_____

84

The #UniversalDesignMethod helps people reframe their thinking, giving them the freedom to shift their paradigm. A #change in physical patterns triggers a shift in mental patterns.

_____

_____

_____

85

The #UniversalDesignMethod helps people see things differently by altering the lenses they use to view things around them. #newmindset

_____

_____

_____

86

The #UniversalDesignMethod creates a new environment for people to experience a shift in #mindset. This paradigm shift can open up volumes of opportunities.

87

Practitioners of the #UniversalDesignMethod benefit from embracing a #newmindset that allows them to find the joy of the journey.

88

When people create a #newmindset, their fears of the future fade, and they are able to appreciate the moment they are in right now.

_____

_____

_____

89

When people give thought to a new way of functioning within their lives, a breakthrough happens. This is an exciting discovery for your journey! #newmindset

_____

_____

_____

After people change their atmosphere, they open themselves up to new #opportunities that can take them on a journey to a happier & healthier path.

LAURA MINEFF
https://Aha.pub/BeARoundPeg

Share the AHA messages from this book socially by going to
https://aha.pub/BeARoundPeg.

Scan the QR code or use this link to watch the section videos and more on this section topic:
https://aha.pub/BeARoundPegSVs

SECTION V

Change your atmosphere so you can see new opportunities.

Think again about physical design and imagine you are house hunting.

You walk into a house, only to be met immediately by a wall. You love everything else about the place and decide to buy the house, but only if you can safely remove that wall. You find out that not only can you do it, but also by doing so, you will now see through to the main living area and more light will come into that room. The entire atmosphere of the house changes as the entryway is opened up.

The atmosphere of our lives is the same. That is the reason that we need to break down our barriers. You just have to ease open the door so you can see where you want to go next. Envision what it will look like without that wall that is a barrier for you.

You can create your own reality. There are no limits.

Allow me another design example.

When you use the same color on your floor and on your walls, you lose perspective. This can be problematic to those with depth perception or balance issues. It is easy to correct. With a simple modification of making one surface darker than the other, you will see the distinction clearly. In design, coloration is used to move you, to calm you, and to inspire you. That in turn, changes the atmosphere further, allowing you to find joy and love in the space where you live and where you work.

Changing your atmosphere allows you to see and do things differently. Altering the ambiance helps shift your mindset.

With a new mindset, you are now ready to set out on your life journey, one that will uncover a number of interesting opportunities for you. It can and will change your life. You will also enhance the lives of those you encounter along the way, expanding the universe together.

You will be able to enjoy the full array of possibilities by integrating beauty and color into your environment and into your life.

By embracing the Universal Design Method, you are empowered to break down barriers, exposing unanticipated opportunities and even your weaknesses. Push through, prevail, embrace, and be proud of yourself.

By altering your atmosphere through this methodology, the world opens up and your reality expands!

The Universal Design Method is all about opening your mind and redesigning both your environment and your lifestyle. It provides a new lens to see your physical spaces and to help discover a new outlook—your new path.

90

When people experience a breakthrough, they start to see things differently. They start to appreciate the atmosphere that they have surrounded themselves with in a new light. #newmindset

---

91

Beautiful #opportunities come to people all the time! They just need to ease open the door of their hearts to see that they are worthy of these opportunities.

92

When people ask for what they want and then let it go, #opportunities will always appear before them. This will bring them closer to what it is that they are asking for. Ask and you shall receive #miracles.

93

Fear can subside when people change their atmosphere. They are able to see opportunities because they are no longer focused on fear. #newmindset

---

94

People must be specific about what they want, so they can be prepared to see the #opportunities. What specific desires do you have?

_____

_____

_____

95

When people have a closed mindset and stick only to exactly what it is that they want, they may miss other #opportunities that are available. But life experiences will continue to help.

_____

_____

_____

96

By altering their atmosphere through the #UniversalDesignMethod, the world opens up and one's reality expands!

97

Learning how to drop the barriers that are blocking people from #change will provide freedom. A free-flowing curved environment can help open up the barriers in their minds, and allow them to become a round peg in a square world.

98

Through a change in atmosphere, people will discover that they can have a new way of life. The #UniversalDesignMethod helps break down the barriers of a person's mind, and exciting #opportunities will be exposed.

99

It is really about what drives people to make a change. By altering the atmosphere through the #UniversalDesignMethod, they will start seeing the #opportunity to do things in a creative and fun way!

_____

_____

_____

100

An amazing transformation takes place when people allow themselves to take advantage of the #opportunities around them. All that is needed is a change of perspective incited by the #UniversalDesignMethod.

_____

_____

_____

101

When people encounter a catalyst, they start making adjustments in their lives. This causes a fun domino effect of #opportunities!

_____

_____

_____

102

After people change their atmosphere, they open themselves up to new #opportunities that can take them on a journey to a happier and healthier path.

_____

_____

_____

> People need to smile at themselves in the mirror every morning & be excited for whatever the day may bring to find #joy. They need to hang onto that feeling of joy & be able to recreate it at any moment.

LAURA MINEFF
https://Aha.pub/BeARoundPeg

Share the AHA messages from this book socially by going to
https://aha.pub/BeARoundPeg.

Scan the QR code or use this link to watch the section videos and more on this section topic:
https://aha.pub/BeARoundPegSVs

SECTION VI

Finding joy in your journey.

When you invoke a memory or you have a life-changing experience, a chemical reaction can occur — the production of Serotonin. This impacts your energy and levels of mood, anxiety, and happiness.

Often, one of our earliest memories is our safety net, our "blankie."

If you close your eyes and reminisce your own baby blanket, in your mind's eye, you may envision the color and experience the feel of the fibers and the freshness right after Mom washed it (or your personal scent if you didn't allow her to wash it). You may even remember the feeling of connection, comfort, and joy that it provided.

That memory represents pure love and an open heart, both of which generate positive energy.

In design, when we touch something, experiencing the texture and the feel, the resulting energy is called "the hand." Using the sense of touch as the primary sense, the hand communicates the messages to the brain and lets us know what sensors are being tapped, including our memories.

So, what is joy, and how do we infuse it into our journey?

Sometimes our mindset tricks us into believing that it is external or situational "things" that will produce joy — the red sportscar, getting engaged, taking a cruise, or receiving a promotion.

The truth is that we achieve joy by focusing on breaking through the barriers of fear and our protective cocoon so we can appreciate how beautiful we are. We can then experience good, loving, warm, and fuzzy feelings about ourselves. At that point, we can embrace and reflect joy back into the universe.

Think again of renovating a house.

You envision the finished product and the joy you will experience, but to get there, it is a process. First, you have to knock down walls, clean up the debris, and then build the new environment. Through the journey, you may experience frustration, but you can also choose to be excited. Your attitude will impact the progress and the outcome, as well as the overall experience. When you are finished with all the elements—paint, carpet, new furnishings—and if you allow your frustration to get to you, you may just want to pay the bill and be done with it, or you can experience true joy and then throw a party to celebrate with others. It is your choice.

To initiate your internal renewal experience, you start with envisioning happiness, then you look forward and create the exciting outcome in your mind's eye. The journey will feel simple and pleasurable if you focus on happiness first. If instead you expect the joy to come if you work hard enough to achieve the outcome or manifestation, your journey will be one of great challenge, like pushing a wet noodle up a hill.

Which path would you choose? Most would prefer to choose the path of least resistance.

When we experience true joy, we are exhilarated. Sometimes we get goosebumps. When it happens, you cannot help but smile. It is like sunshine flowing through your body. It warms and cuddles you.

Joy lets you see things with a new mindset and expands your world.

There is joy in every journey. Enjoying the adventure begins with the appreciation of the simple things around you, such as the sunshine and the fact that it's a new morning. Joy may be as simple as the smell of coffee or the taste of great chocolate. But most importantly, it involves acknowledging and appreciating yourself.

Embracing that unbridled joy allows us to experience (and create) the manifestation of the desires of our heart.

As you progress through your life journey, when you show appreciation for things that happen to you, that gratitude opens up your whole heart. You can't help but learn what it means to love without condition.

Joy radiates from giving and receiving that pure, unconditional love. It is an expression of the internal beauty of who we are. You can then truly appreciate yourself and your contribution to this great and wonderful universe. It then becomes our desire to share that discovery with others.

Adopting the Universal Design Method customizes your atmosphere to reflect who you truly are. It helps you find your joy so you can make healthy steps forward in your loving and joyful life.

Your memories of the happy places in your life can become fuel for you, as you remember and smile. At any time, you can recall the power and joy of the moment.

It is already within you.

103

The #joy is in the journey of opening up to new things and taking that happier and healthier next step in life.

_____

_____

_____

104

#Joy is irresistible and does not have to be explained. People only need to trust in the loving joy of life.

_____

_____

_____

105

#Joy happens when one cannot help but smile.
It is like sunshine that flows through one's
body—like warm cuddles.

_____

_____

_____

106

People need to smile at themselves in the mirror every
morning and be excited for whatever the day may bring
to find #joy. They need to hang onto that feeling of joy
and be able to recreate it at any moment.

_____

_____

_____

107

#Joy radiates from giving and receiving pure, unconditional love. In finding joy, people can expect exhilaration and the feeling where they get goosebumps. The ability to conjure this feeling at any time is the key to life's happiness.

_____

_____

_____

108

With big things and AHA moments, goosebumps happen when people connect to the #oneness and open up to the realization that everyone is connected to each other. We are all in this #together. #change

_____

_____

_____

109

Finding #joy is finding the thing that gives one goosebumps and getting them every day. What gives you goosebumps?

_____

_____

_____

110

When things no longer bring #joy to one's life, it is time to hand it off to someone else. The joy is now in letting go and moving on.

_____

_____

_____

111

Instead of looking for #joy, people must allow it into their lives. This requires letting go and letting love and appreciation into their lives.

_____

_____

_____

112

Finding #joy is in the enthusiasm of working, creating, loving, and sharing together. Have you found your joy?

_____

_____

_____

113

When people feel the love and #joy and serenity of life,
they explode with the desire to share and give in any
way they can.

_____

_____

_____

114

#Joy becomes everyone's motivation to participate in a
much bigger way than anyone even thinks is possible.
How are you participating in the life
events around you?

_____

_____

_____

115

The #joy of sharing love, happiness, and well-being brings people healing. Have you shared your joy today?

116

#Joy sparks excitement in people and opens them up to collaboration with others.

117

When people find #joy, they find the inspiration to give back and contribute to society in a way that is vital to life. Be a deliberate creator.

_____

_____

_____

118

Finding #joy lets people see things with a new mindset. It expands their world and allows love to flow. The #UniversalDesignMethod creates physical spaces for expansion and energy flow.

_____

_____

_____

119

#Joy is contagious! Tune in and tap into joy.
Inspiration is a choice. When people use the
#UniversalDesignMethod in their surroundings, they can
find inspiration all around them.

_____

_____

_____

120

Tuning into the #joy of what one is doing opens them up
to the true meaning of the journey that they are on. The
#UniversalDesignMethod can help people find meaning
through a shift in thinking.

_____

_____

_____

121

When people find #joy, synergy takes off and creativity is released. The #UniversalDesignMethod helps unleash creativity by helping people find joy in their homes and workplaces, in the daily routine of life.

122

When people have the opportunity to venture into new concepts, they get excited and find #joy. The #UniversalDesignMethod can inspire people to go on new adventures.

123

People must have a daily appreciation of something in their world. Through this appreciation, they find the true connection of their love and happiness with the greater being.

_____

_____

_____

124

In order to allow #joy into life, people must find one thing to be appreciative of every morning and before going to bed. #mantra

_____

_____

_____

125

Once people become appreciative, their whole heart will open up. They will appreciate themselves and the world around them. This is the key to true bliss. What have you appreciated today? #joy

_____

_____

_____

126

When people find the #joy in their journey, it gives them the courage to move forward and venture into a happier and healthier life.

_____

_____

_____

Life is all about the #journey & the destination is just a great excuse. Remember to enjoy your journey to a happier & healthier, loving life.

LAURA MINEFF

https://Aha.pub/BeARoundPeg

Share the AHA messages from this book socially by going to
https://aha.pub/BeARoundPeg.

Scan the QR code or use this link to watch the section videos and more on this section topic:
https://aha.pub/BeARoundPegSVs

SECTION VII

What's next? It's time to make a new plan.

You evolve as you go through your life's journey. Your story will change over time, and you need to learn how to tell that story to reflect your evolution and to present and project who you have become.

When you become one with your identity, knowledge, and self-worth, you become one with your life.

You also need to hear the stories of others to appreciate them. When we are able to truly hear and accept the truth of and honor their backstories, only then can we really come together and create a shift in the paradigm.

You now have the tools that you need to make this happen. You are equipped to be inspired and incorporate what you've learned about each aspect of your journey. You can reveal and extend your love and joy to those who cross your path, even those who were a part of your early conditioning. You benefit others by offering the learning from your journey, which adds to your joy.

When you are tuned into your happiness, joy, and love, it goes out to everyone. Ultimately, it is all about the journey and the adventures along the way. You have the pleasure and tools to manifest whatever you desire.

Now you know how to tune in and tap into that perfect gift that you received when you entered this life.

Within your reach are all the dreams, all the joy, and all the love that you desire. You have permission to reach in and connect at any time to the power source and the positive energy of unconditional love.

Incorporating the Universal Design Method adds value to your life by giving you a fresh new outlook, influenced by the energy flow of your new environment. You get to be a part of painting your own canvas.

You will find appreciation for where you have come from and where you are today. Through this renewed outlook, you will experience a desire to enhance how you interact with society as a whole.

Applying the Universal Design Methodology awakens you to infinite possibilities that you can choose, using joy and love as the fuel.

My desire for you is that you would enjoy the wonder of being a round peg in our square world.

127

Every door of opportunity opens when people move aside their fear and find courage to see things differently. This allows them to #journey to a happier and healthier life!

128

Catalysts propel people to find the courage to change their direction in life. This puts them on the #journey to appreciating themselves. One's environment is a critical part of self-discovery.

129

When people are on the #journey of reinventing themselves, the next step is to find ways to reinsert themselves into society and participate in enhancing society as a whole.

_____

_____

_____

130

When people become one with their identity, knowledge, and expertise, they become one with their lives. They are now at a point where they can give back to society. #journey

_____

_____

_____

131

When people finally tap into the bliss in their own
path that is unique to them, they find the desire to help
others find their own unique #journey in life.

_____

_____

_____

132

People can add value to others by offering their
#journey as an enhancement to society as a whole. An
enhanced atmosphere touches all who live in it.

_____

_____

_____

133

A new mindset can guide people toward a new direction in their lives. Doors open up for people to choose the next step. The beginning of the new #journey can be refreshing and rewarding.

_____

_____

_____

134

People gain wisdom and knowledge along the #journey. The #UniversalDesignMethod reflects that enlightenment through what is expressed in one's home and workplace.

_____

_____

_____

135

When people extend the learning from their #journey and share it to society, they become the ultimate receiver, exploding with the power of joy. The #UniversalDesignMethod revolves around allowing the environment to evolve with you.

136

Giving back is facilitating, mentoring, and co-working with the universe as a whole. The #UniversalDesignMethod is all about co-creating your environment. #journey

---

137

Whatever joy people have found along their journey is the feeling they need to recreate and what they need to share to the world. The #UniversalDesignMethod allows them to share in that experience. #journey.

_____

_____

_____

138

Along people's #journey, they often find others who are going in the same direction. We draw like-minded people to us. This encourages more connections and more people participating in the enhancement of the evolution of the world.

_____

_____

_____

139

The #journey of finding joy leads to a multitude of opportunities. What opportunities have opened up for you?

_____

_____

_____

140

Life is all about the #journey and the destination is just a great excuse. Remember to enjoy your journey to a happier and healthier, loving life.

_____

_____

_____

EPILOGUE

I was a brand-new mom. I was also curious and loved seeing how other people lived.

My dad was a fireman and a builder. We lived plainly, with no extras. My mom was stay-at-home, while my dad provided; it was very traditional. We did not have cellphones. We didn't have the internet. We didn't have an HDTV. There was no Martha Stewart.

Yet in the midst of it all, I had this desire, and I didn't know what to do with it. I also had a new catalyst in my life, which was my new baby, bringing me so much love and joy.

I had a yearning to find a way to connect to myself.

I would go on walks with my little girl through the neighborhood. Many homes in the neighborhood didn't have garages. I would stand on the sidewalk and try to look into other people's homes. I would even go at night because most people would have their lights on and their windows open, and I could see inside.

I soon found out that they had open houses for homes that were for sale. So, for three hours every Sunday, I would go to as many open houses as I could manage.

I frequently saw the same realtor. She finally looked at me and said, "Look, I don't know what you're doing, but I know you're not going to buy a house. Could you please just go get your real estate license?" That prompted me to ask, "I could do that?" She answered, "Yeah, three weekends, John Honduras. Just go do it because I'm trying to get clients here and you're taking up my time." So, I thought, "This is awesome!"

Within three weeks, I signed up and got my real estate license.

Then, I became the open house guru.

Epilogue

Had the real estate agent not said something, I wouldn't have known that I could even go down this path. That literally started opening doors for me. You might say that she was my next catalyst.

As I saw all these homes that were on the market, I asked myself, "What can I do to help these people and other realtors see the potential and create a desire to live in these homes and make it their own?"

So, I got a bucket and rags. I got 40-watt light bulbs and candles to create a welcoming, homey atmosphere.

I would call the homeowner before I'd have their open house and say, "Hey, listen. I know you're excited to find your new home and get ready to move. I'm going to hold your open house. Would you be willing to leave me a few boxes? Would it be all right if I just started to declutter and pack a few things up for you? I'll label the boxes carefully, so you'll know exactly what I've put in them." And people would say, "Sure, no problem."

I would go an hour ahead of time to my open house. I would wash the fingerprints off the woodwork and clean all the tables. I would either pop a frozen pumpkin pie in the oven or at least make a few slices of raisin-bread toast.

I touched all the senses, including sound—with low happy music, not elevator sounds. I would rearrange their furniture, shifting the energy.

I would simplify things so those coming to see the home could envision and imagine it as their own.

After I had held their open house, when the homeowners would come home, I would have at least two people interested in purchasing their home. Sometimes, I'd already have an offer. As a bonus, the owners would have a clean and decluttered house, giving them a head start on their moving process.

I invented the first staging. Today, people make it a career. But the cool part was watching the homeowners come home, be surprised, and say, "We don't even want to move now."

They had no idea that this change was possible, because they had become so habitual about their living and how they utilized their home. I didn't do anything except rearrange what they already had and create a new atmosphere for them.

From there, I went full force into helping people envision what their life could look like.

I helped them open up those doors of opportunity so they could take the next step into wherever they were going. I created an atmosphere that allowed them to see different opportunities. I loved seeing and being a part of their joy and their excitement.

Life went on. I had more children, and then I got divorced, which was my new catalyst. After that, I had to see my own life and future differently.

I started with corporate gift packaging. My sister helped me with this business. I loved being creative with her, but we had no money. So, we would go to garage sales and thrift stores. We would gather whatever we could for a small amount of money and put these amazing things into themed baskets together. I sold them to banks and realtors who were giving them to their employees and clients.

Our business was growing, and we were working out of my home. People who came into my home to get the baskets would say, "Wow, I love those window treatments. Could you make those for me?" So, I started thinking that we should just have an open house with all these cool fun things that we found and refurbished. We could sell them!

I started having these open houses once a week. I was willing to sell everything in my house. I was a single mom of four children with minimal support.

People would line up out the door at 7 am and buy my stuff. At one point, my kids commented that if it wasn't nailed down, it might get sold! This helped them to develop into young people who were not materialistic.

Every week, after we would have these open houses, we would begin again on Monday and collect new items. Finally, people started inviting me into their homes and asking me if I could do the same thing for them.

I'd go into their homes and do exactly what I used to do for the open houses. I would go to discount stores and then take off all the labels, so they didn't know how much things cost. I'd write up a price sheet, and people would buy everything that I put in there.

These were mostly picture frames and small things. It just escalated from there, and people started asking me to participate in designing their homes.

That was all the basis for my development of the Universal Design Method.

The system works.

Every door of opportunity included me moving aside the fear, letting go, and having the courage to see things differently.

I've lived my life that way. And you can too.

Be the round peg in your square world.

ABOUT THE AUTHOR

LAURA MINEFF is a lifestyle designer who has owned and operated her business, Array Design Studio, for over twenty years.

During those years, she grew to listen and understand from her clients what they needed to better their lives. From that experience, she created the Universal Design Method (UDM).

Laura now uses her method to infuse happiness into the lives of her clients. She saw the need to share these methods with others in the industry, as well as the average person. It was her heart's desire to make UDM accessible to all. This is how she came to write this book and share those methods with you.

She currently lives Cleveland, Ohio, where she is working on a multi-use community that will be designed around the UDM. You can also catch her series, *Laura Mineff: Lifestyle Designer*, on YouTube, where she takes you through all the processes of UDM. Additionally, she is starting a UDM academy for those interested in getting a full Universal Design Method experience.

If you'd like to find out more about the projects Laura is working on or to be more involved in her academy, please go to LauraMineff.com or find her on Facebook and Instagram @LauraMineffLifestyleDesigner.

AHA**that**®

THiNKaha has created AHAthat for you to share content from this book.

➲ Share each AHA message socially: **https://aha.pub/BeARoundPeg**

➲ Share additional content: **https://AHAthat.com**

➲ Info on authoring: **https://AHAthat.com/Author**

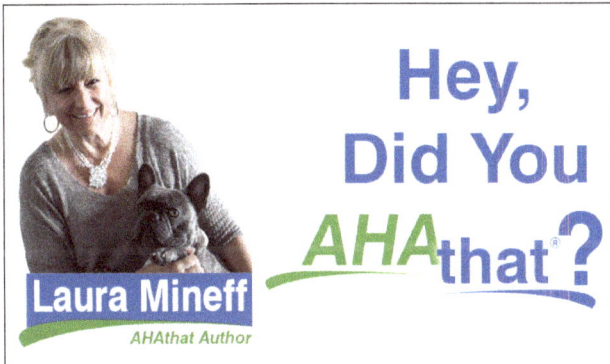
Hey, Did You AHA**that**®?

Laura Mineff
AHAthat Author

.

www.ingramcontent.com/pod-product-compliance
Lightning Source LLC
Chambersburg PA
CBHW040805150426
42813CB00056B/2653